HEART BEAT

noun
1: one complete pulsation of the heart as it pumps blood
2: the vital center or driving impulse
3: a brief space of time: without any delay or hesitation—
used chiefly in the phrase *in a heartbeat.*

Doe Boyle

illustrated by
Daniel Long

Albert Whitman & Company
Chicago, Illinois

The heart is an organ.
It works like a pump.
It pushes blood throughout the body.

The heart pumps—or beats—all the time.
It beats when the body is awake.
It beats when the body is asleep.
It pulses in concert with the earliest stirrings of life.
And, in creatures with hearts, each life ends at the moment it stops.

A heartbeat is the unmistakable sound of a tireless muscle.
It is the measured throb at the core of many living creatures.
Lub-dub. Lub-dub. Lub-dub.

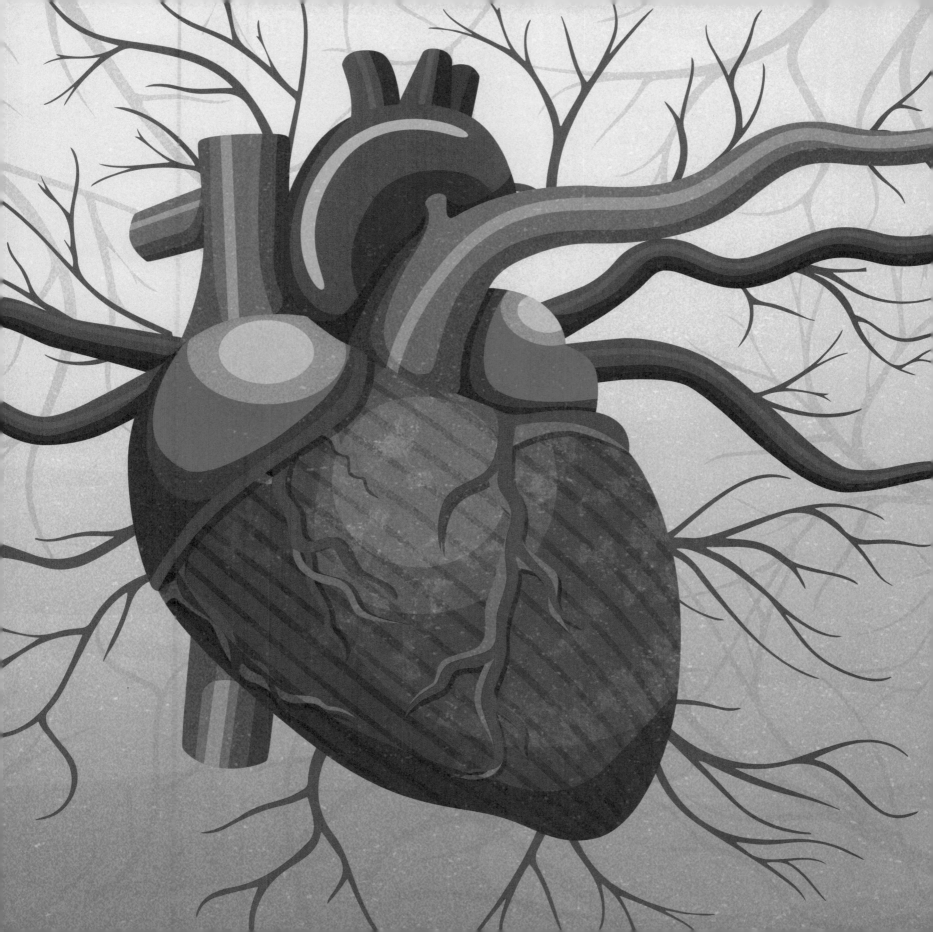

The heart of a pygmy shrew—
a white-toothed, fleet-footed Etruscan shrew—
beats fifteen hundred times each minute.

Fast as a flash—*flick-dash*, *flick-dash*—deep in the thickets,
feasting in a fever, out on the grasslands—
twitch-snatch, *twitch-snatch*—gulping down ants.

Twenty-five times—yes, twenty-five times—in each teeny second,
from daybreak to starlight
and *back round, back round, back round AGAIN*!

A pygmy shrew is thought to have
the world's fastest heart rate.

Its super-sensitive whiskers let the
shrew know when it brushes against
an insect, which it quickly eats.

The pygmy shrew must eat nearly twice its own we ght every day for energy.

The heart of a hummer beats less than that shrew's.
A thousand *lub-dubs* each minute will do.
Flit-flit, flit-flit.
Hoverrrrrrr. Rest.
Flit-flit, flit-flit.
Hoverrrrrrr. Rest.

Its heartbeat hammers; its tiny chest drums
on twig and bud
in nest, in flight.
A million-plus thumps,
at dawn, at night.

One million four hundred thousand-plus beats
each twenty-four hours.
Flit-flit, flit-flit.
Every single day.

A hummingbird's heart
can beat 1,260 times a
minute when it's flying.

It needs to eat a lot, for energy, to keep its wings beating fast and to fly long distances.

Hummingbirds sip flower nectar and eat pollen, gnats, midges, aphids, and flies.

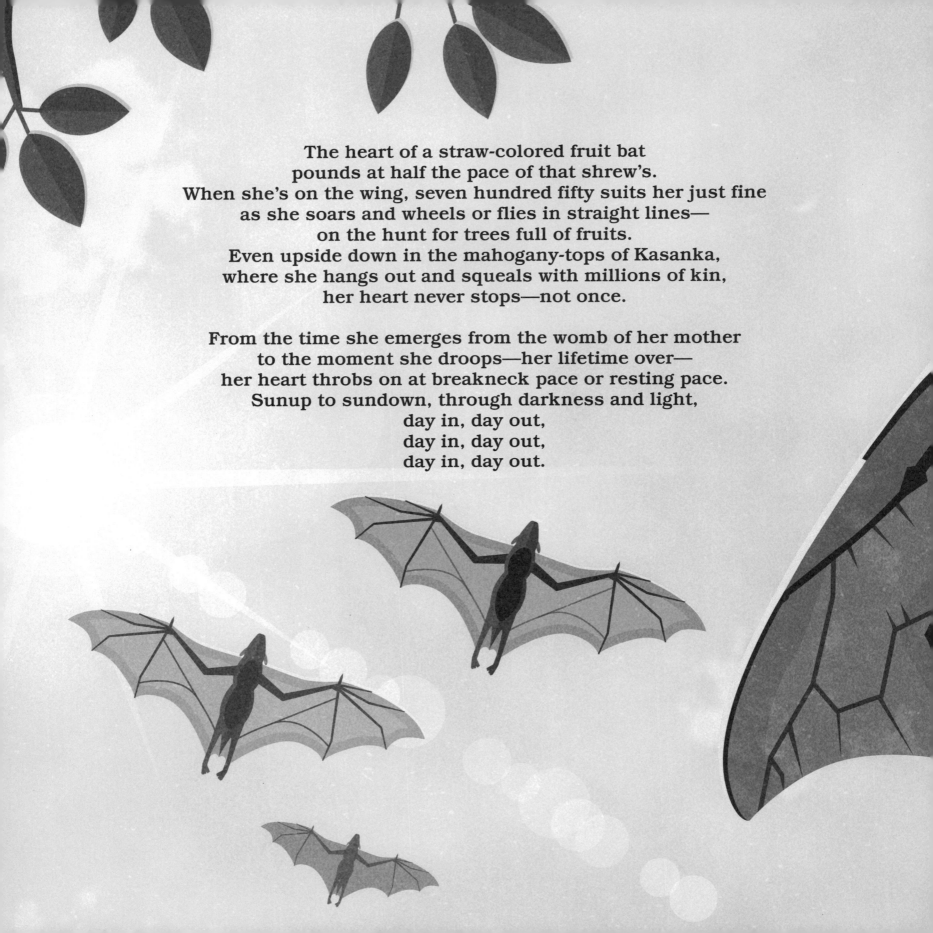

The heart of a straw-colored fruit bat
pounds at half the pace of that shrew's.
When she's on the wing, seven hundred fifty suits her just fine
as she soars and wheels or flies in straight lines—
on the hunt for trees full of fruits.
Even upside down in the mahogany-tops of Kasanka,
where she hangs out and squeals with millions of kin,
her heart never stops—not once.

From the time she emerges from the womb of her mother
to the moment she droops—her lifetime over—
her heart throbs on at breakneck pace or resting pace.
Sunup to sundown, through darkness and light,
day in, day out,
day in, day out,
day in, day out.

This bat can migrate farther than most mammals, traveling thousands of miles each year.

It has a large heart for its size, to power its wings for its long-distance flights.

Fruit bats live in huge social colonies, with up to almost one million animals.

Kasanka National Park is in Zambia, where up to 10 million of these bats live from October to December every year.

The heart of a meadow mouse pounds slower by far.
This little ticker pumps five hundred times plus thirty more beats
in every slim minute in every full day—except in winter.

For twelve solid hours, from midnight to noon,
then back round to midnight for twelve hours more,
this heart drums on, not fast, not slow.
Just right. Just right. Just right. Just right.

And then in winter? It beats a good bit slower:
Just   right.
Just   right.
Just   right.

This jumping mouse, often called a
field mouse, is one of only four mammals in
North America that hibernate.

Along with the woodchuck, the little brown
bat, and the woodland jumping mouse, it falls into
deep sleep from October to April.

In its burrow, it breathes just a few breaths per
minute, its body temperature drops, and its heart
rate slows to just five beats per minute.

The heart of a giraffe,
specially built for a skyscraping brain,
beats one hundred-fifty times each minute—each *minute*!—
just to be sure that no giraffe faints.

It's a mighty tall order for a two-foot heart
weighing twenty-five pounds,
but it keeps its beat, its beat—that beat!—
while big hand and small hand circle the clock.

It moves the blood through a net of valves
for the blood rambling up
and the blood rushing down
the towering neck
of a tree-grazing, leaf-nuzzling, knobby-skulled head.

The giraffe has an unusually long neck—and so its heart lies very far below its brain.

When the giraffe lowers its head, its blood rushes downward toward its brain. To keep the giraffe from fainting, a net of arteries and veins in its neck slows down the blood.

When the giraffe lifts its head, the net redirects the blood into the brain. No fainting!

The heart of a mountain gorilla
thumps seventy times each minute—
give or take a few—or five—beats.
Not much different from other great apes.

In and out of seasons
and around the clock,
while tumbling and tackling their sisters and brothers
or nursing rich milk in the arms of their mothers,
little gorillas (and older ones too)
have hearts with arteries, chambers, and valves,
and pulses that vary throughout the day,
whether scared or at peace or asleep or at play.

In the wild, gorillas live for about 35
years. They live in small groups called
troops, and they care for one another.

Gorillas have hands and feet like
humans, and they use their fingers
in the same ways. They also have
unique, individual fingerprints.

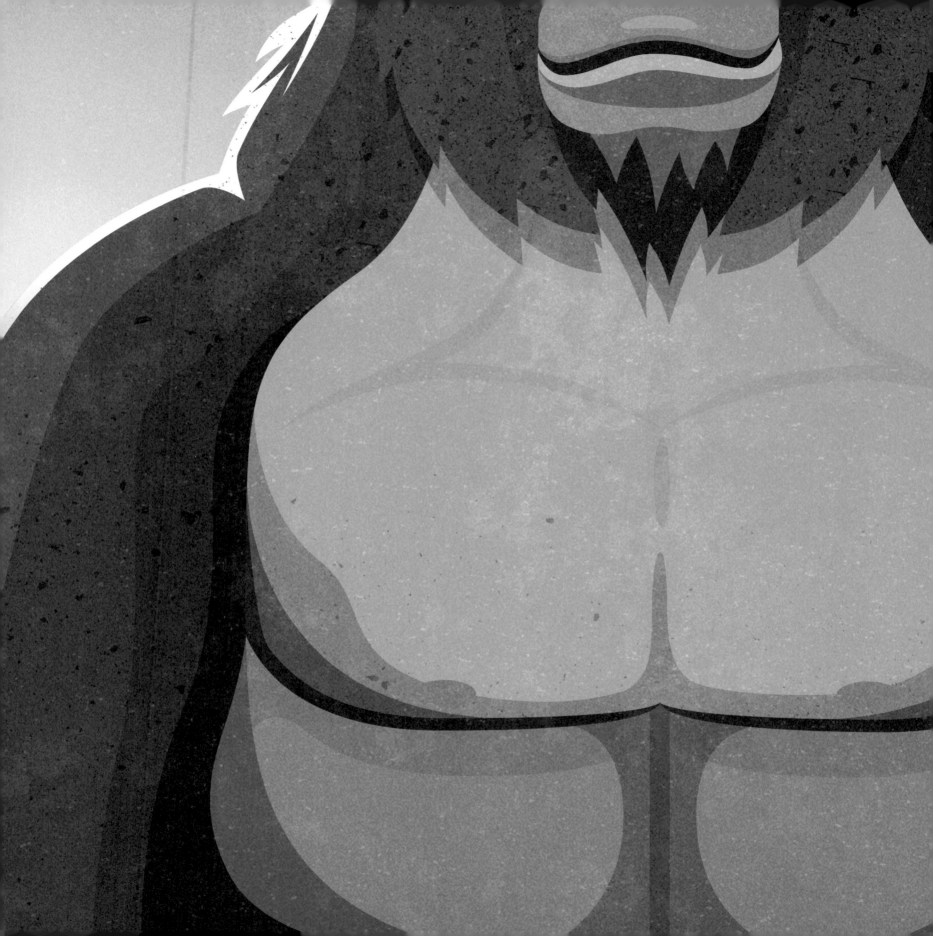

The hearts—all three—of an octopus
have a mammal-like pattern—*lub-dub*, *lub-dub*—
like that of all creatures whose blood needs pumping.

Forty-odd beats in each and every minute
is often spot-on for this spineless critter
—but it all depends:
Is he fleeing or hunting? Is she swimming or crawling?
In cold-ish water? Or something less cool?

Four times ten might slow right down—
slow waaaay waaaay down—
to NO beats at all from time to time.
Year in, year out.
Year in.
Year…
Out.

The octopus has three separate hearts. One pumps blood throughout its body, and two pump blood across the octopus's two gills, through which it breathes.

At certain times, the heart that pumps blood through its body stops. No beats at all. This can happen when the octopus is swimming with jet propulsion instead of crawling or gliding.

The heart of a camel likes a leisurely pace.
Thirty beats a minute make sense for this beast.
Rocking and rolling through sand and storm,
the camel is a mammal with a heart untaxed.
The camel is a mammal with its heart relaxed.

Under the sun, under the moon,
sleeping near a tent on the banks of the Nile,
its heart stays steady as the river flows by.
But racing cross the desert on the road to Khartoum,
its heart thumps faster while the sand flies high.
Under the sun, under the stars,
camels rest easy in oases and bazaars.

Of all land mammals, a camel may
have the slowest heart rate when
resting. But when the camel is
working, its heart rate can climb to
almost 60 beats per minute.

The heart of a python, who's hidden in swamplands,
beats at just the right pace for a sit-and-wait snake.
Twenty-five times per minute is plenty,
when it's sunning or sleeping, and its belly is empty.
Lub-dub. Lub-dub.
Sorta slow.

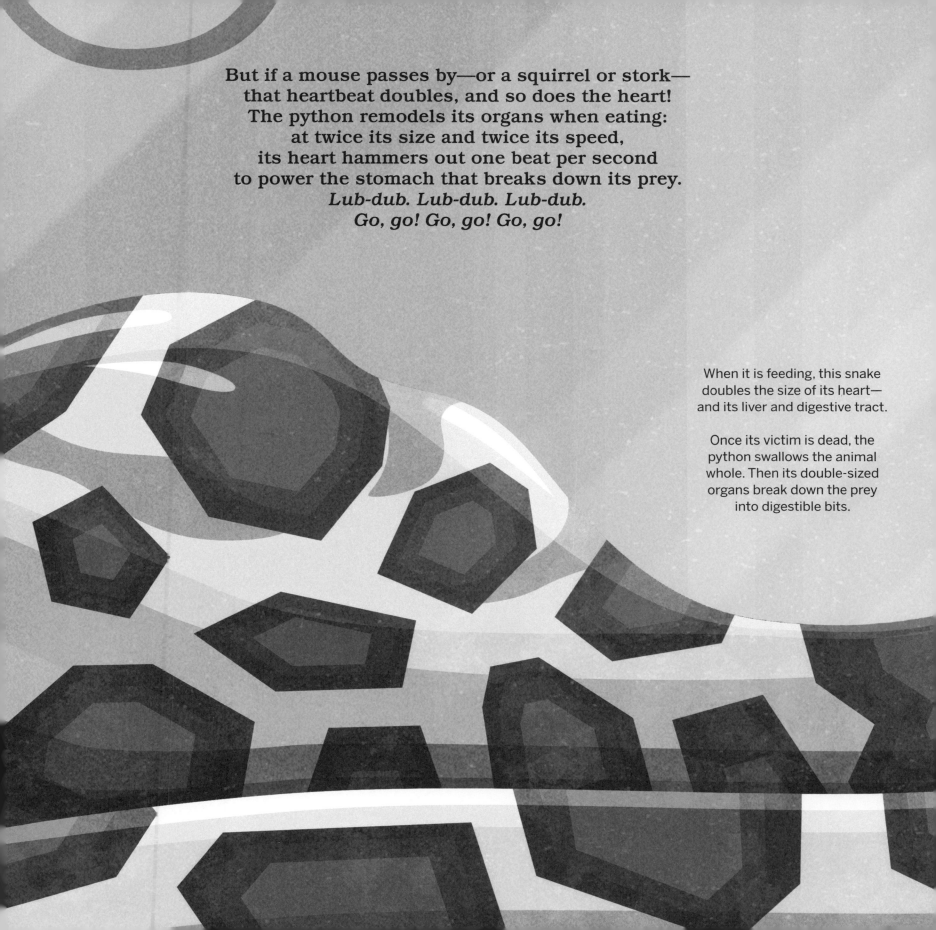

But if a mouse passes by—or a squirrel or stork—
that heartbeat doubles, and so does the heart!
The python remodels its organs when eating:
at twice its size and twice its speed,
its heart hammers out one beat per second
to power the stomach that breaks down its prey.
Lub-dub. Lub-dub. Lub-dub.
Go, go! Go, go! Go, go!

When it is feeding, this snake
doubles the size of its heart—
and its liver and digestive tract.

Once its victim is dead, the
python swallows the animal
whole. Then its double-sized
organs break down the prey
into digestible bits.

The heart of a blue whale
beats eight times a minute.
Or ten, sometimes—or six or even just two when diving.
Every day. All day.
Breeching. Logging.
Filling with krill.

Eight huge heartbeats
in every peaceful minute,
at dawn, at dusk,
and back round again.

Surely not fast,
but not too slow.
The perfect pace—
for a giant of a whale.

The huge heart of an adult blue whale is the largest heart of any living animal.

With help from its heart, a blue whale mother produces at least 50 gallons of milk daily to feed its calf, which gains 9 pounds an hour.

In evergreen forests of the great Far North
live black-masked wood frogs,
whom you might hear chuckling
(like a quacking duckling)
in springtime and summer and fall.

But you won't hear them or see them once winter comes,
when they nestle deep into the forest-floor litter.
There, undercover, they freeze ice-cube solid.
These frozen froggies lie rigid and still;
their heartbeats quelled by near-arctic chill.
Silent and stony, they never hop—
how could they, when their heartbeats stop?

When the weather warms up, those quackers defrost,
with their hearts pushing blood just four beats per minute.
And when they have thawed, they head back to the pond
to make new broods of tadpoles—a thousand or more—
who can tell they are kin
by their scent or their shape or the spots on their skin.

The tiny heart of a wood frog is truly slow. Its
resting heart rate is just four beats a minute.

In cold climates, a wood frog's heart can stop
completely in winter—for up to eight months!

As freezing begins, the frog's heart rate doubles
to eight beats per minute—and then stops.
Motionless, breathless, the frog remains rock
solid until March or April.

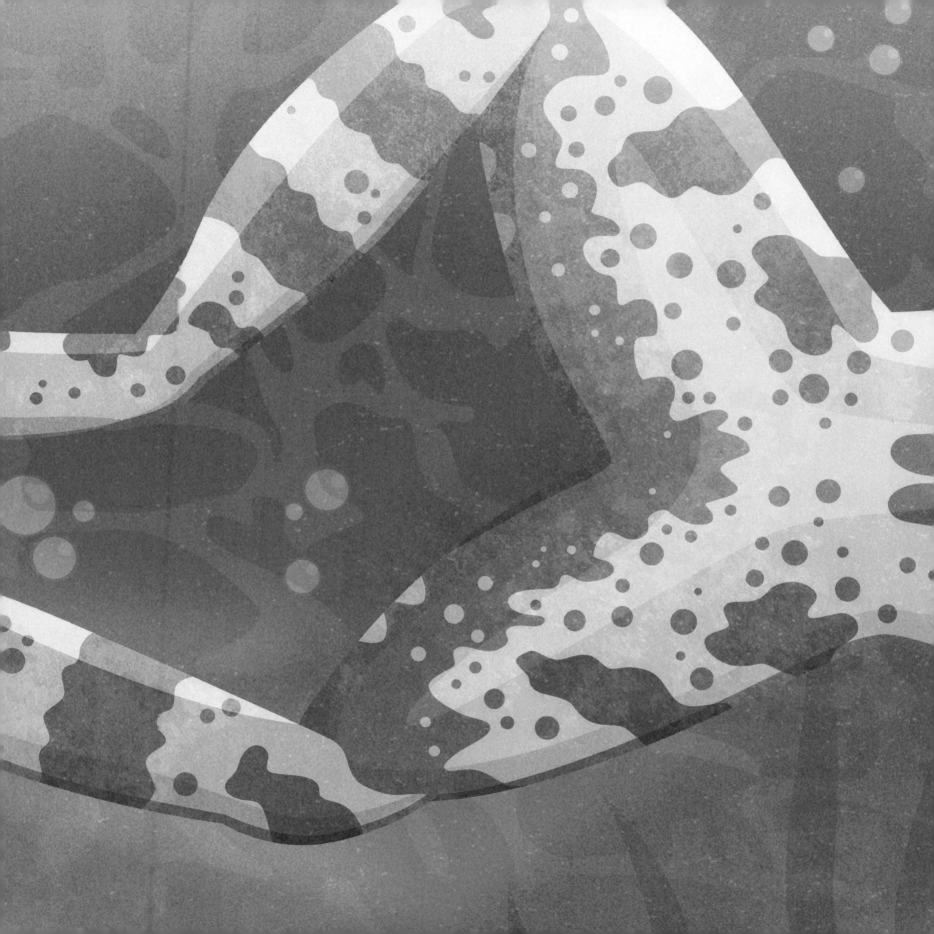

But what about *you*?
What does *your* heart do?

The heart of a human, when it's full grown,
beats seventy times—or a few beats more or perhaps a few less—
in each little minute that its person's at rest.
Every day. All day. Day in. Day out.
Two billion beats in each human lifetime of eighty-plus years—
plus half a billion more if we reach one hundred.

An infant is born with a heart that ticks faster by far
than the grown-ups who gather to welcome its birth.
Each baby's heart throbs one hundred-fifty times
—or a few beats less or a handful more—
in each resting minute.
Then, with each day that passes till we are age one,
our heart rate slows,
hugging one hundred beats in each precious minute.

The ticker of a toddler—and later a teen—
might beat close to eighty times a minute at rest
and near ninety at play—so just the right pace
for the size of someone who's growing.
While we dream through the night or run down the field,
our hearts drum on—
lub-dub lub-dub lub-dub.

We have steady rhythms, slow and fast,
for days of ease and days more speedy.
Days in. Days out.
Sunrise to sunset and back round again.
Lub-dub. Lub-dub.
Soft as a sigh or thunderous as a storm,
as we sleep and play
and rest and work
and love one another
throughout our days.
Lub-dub. Lub-dub. Lub-dub.

How Your Heart Works

Your heart is a muscle about the size of an adult fist. It expands and contracts around 100,000 times each day. Each expansion and contraction is one heartbeat.

Your heart pumps blood around your body through your veins and arteries. Veins carry blood to your heart, and arteries take blood away from your heart. The blood that flows away from the heart brings oxygen and food to every cell in your body, to create energy. The blood also removes waste.

The four hollow chambers in your heart are separated by valves that make sure your blood flows in the right direction. Blood without a lot of oxygen flows into your heart and gets pumped out to your lungs, where it picks up oxygen. The blood with more oxygen then gets pumped through your body.

Your heart has an electrical system that creates your heart rhythm and your heart rate, which is how often your heart beats.

The "lub-dub" sound of your heartbeat is the sound your heart valves make when they close. The "lub" sound happens when the valves between the atria and the ventricles close, stopping blood from flowing backward. The "dub" sound happens when the aortic and pulmonary valves close as your heart pumps blood into your arteries and onward throughout your body.

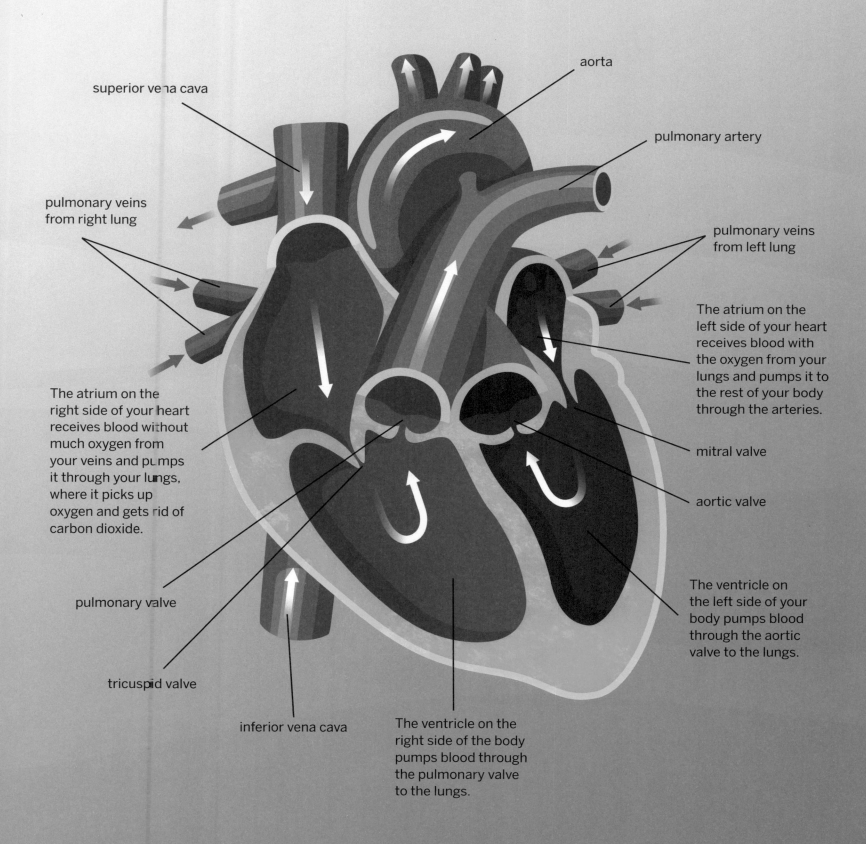

superior vena cava

aorta

pulmonary artery

pulmonary veins
from right lung

pulmonary veins
from left lung

The atrium on the
left side of your heart
receives blood with
the oxygen from your
lungs and pumps it to
the rest of your body
through the arteries.

The atrium on the
right side of your heart
receives blood without
much oxygen from
your veins and pumps
it through your lungs,
where it picks up
oxygen and gets rid of
carbon dioxide.

mitral valve

aortic valve

pulmonary valve

The ventricle on
the left side of your
body pumps blood
through the aortic
valve to the lungs.

tricuspid valve

inferior vena cava

The ventricle on the
right side of the body
pumps blood through
the pulmonary valve
to the lungs.

Author's Note

Heartbeat was born on my back porch. Near my sunny yellow chair, a hummingbird hovered at an open-throated honeysuckle blossom. By my side sat my son-in-law, James Casey, a biologist. Together we held our breaths and watched the tiny bird gather nectar while beating her wings at impossibly high speed. After she sped off, James mentioned that he had just read some new data on hummingbird biology—and on their heart rates in particular. I got to wandering inside of my mind. I got to studying—a summer-long exploration of comparative heart structures and heart rate biologies. The whys and the wherefores. The science and the magic of life here on Earth. This book celebrates the facts that captured my imagination—and my heart.

Resources

books for children

DeGezelle, Terri. *Your Heart*. North Mankato, MN: Capstone, 2002.

LeVert, Suzanne. *The Heart*. New York: Marshall Cavendish, 2001.

Showers, Paul. *A Drop of Blood*. New York: HarperCollins, 2004.

Simon, Seymour. *The Heart: Our Circulatory System*. New York: HarperCollins, 2006.

books for adults

Doyle, Brian. *The Wet Engine: Exploring the Mad Wild Miracle of the Heart*. Brewster, MA: Paraclete, 2005.

Jauhar, Sandeep. *Heart: A History*. New York: Picador, 2019.

For James Patrick Casey, with endless love—DB

For anyone who ever encouraged me to draw—DL

Library of Congress Cataloging-in-Publication data is on file with the publisher.
Text copyright © 2020 Doe Boyle
Illustrations copyright © 2020 by Albert Whitman & Company
Illustrations by Daniel Long
First published in the United States of America in 2020 by Albert Whitman & Company

ISBN 978-0-8075-3190-7 (hardcover)
ISBN 978-0-8075-3191-4 (ebook)

Printed in China

10 9 8 7 6 5 4 3 2 1 WKT 24 23 22 21 20

Design by Rick DeMonico

For more information about Albert Whitman & Company,
visit our website at www.albertwhitman.com